Euripides

Cyclops

Translation by David Bolton

Published by Lulu Books

2019

Copyright by David Bolton

ISBN 978-0-244-22432-5

Terms for the performance of this play may be obtained from
David Bolton at dgbolton0@gmail.com.

All translations in this edition, including the introductory sections (unless
specifically attributed) are by David Bolton.

Colour: Black

Contents

Satyrs and Satyr plays

Homer's *Iliad* and *Odyssey* do not mention Satyrs (Σατύροι) or Silenus (Σιληνός or Σειληνός). There is, however, a single reference to Satyrs in Hesiod, whose works were written c700 BC. The reference is contained in a fragment of the first century AD historian and geographer, Strabo, and is to "the race of worthless Satyrs, suited not for work" [1]. The *Hymn to Aphrodite*, attributed to Homer refers to Sileni (Σειληνοί): "with them [*the Nymphs*], Sileni and the keen-eyed slayer of Argus/ make love in the nooks of charming caves." [2].

The 'Homeric' Hymns were attributed to Homer (as fifth-century BC historian Thucydides attributed the *Hymn to Apollo* to Homer[3]). Their actual authorship and dates are problematic. The *Hymn to Aphrodite* could be seventh or sixth century BC.

The distinction between Satyrs and Sileni is unclear. However, Pausanias says simply "The oldest of the Satyrs are called Sileni" [4]. In *Cyclops*, as elsewhere, Silenus has become the name of one particular member of the Sileni, who refers to the Satyrs as his 'children'.

---

[1] Hesiodi *Carmina* ed. C Göttling Fragment 94, CXXIX: Strabo, X. p. 471 [Hesiod Fr 198.2]

[2] Homer, *Hymn to Aphrodite* 262 – 263

[3] Thucydides, *Histories*, III 104

[4] Pausanias, *Description of Greece* 1. 23. 6

Silenus and his Satyrs are spirits (like the Nymphs they pursue). Images of them can be found in Greek vase paintings of the sixth to the fourth centuries BC. The way Satyrs were depicted changed over time, but generally, Satyrs are shown with bristly hair, snub noses, pointed ears, two small horns, a horse or goat's tail and are often ithyphallic. Sileni, in addition, are elderly with bald heads and beards. Satyrs and Sileni may, to a greater or lesser extent, resemble animals, particularly goats or rams.

Vase painting from the mid-sixth century BC provides evidence for the origins of Greek dramatic comedy generally in the form of depictions of a variety of what are taken to be comic characters. Some characters appear to form choruses dressed as horses, birds and dolphins; others represent everyday people, such as cooks, angry old men and women, and slaves; others again represent Satyrs and Silenus. A Corinthian vase apparently depicts thieves stealing wine; and another depicts gods and heroes, the actors wearing short costumes, padded buttocks and huge phalloi. Vase painting may provide excellent detail, but the lack of explanation accompanying the paintings may lead to wide misinterpretation. The paintings certainly provide no explanation for the different types of character portrayed. There is little written evidence for the origins of the earliest forms of comedy; there are, for example, some fragments of an early form of comedy from Sicily, but little else. The word 'comedy', however, is derived from *kōmos* (κῶμος) a 'revel' and *ōidē* (ᾠδή) a 'song', and the word 'chorus' or *choros* (χορός) means a 'dance' or a 'group of dancers and singers'. Hence, comic choruses may perhaps have arisen originally from songs sung and danced to during feasting and revelling.

8

Although comedies may have been performed in many places, they became best known for their part in the festival of Dionysus, the Dionysia, held in Athens. The tragic poet, Pratinas, is credited in the *Suda* (pi 2230) with introducing Satyr plays to the festival in the year of the seventieth Olympiad, that is, 500 BC. The custom came to be established that tragic poets would present a trilogy of tragic plays followed by a light-hearted Satyr play.

The Satyr plays, like *Cyclops*, seem to have followed a similar format. Each play would take as its theme a well-known mythological story: in *Cyclops*, the story is of Odysseus' encounter with the Cyclops, Polyphemus. Satyrs and their elderly leader, Silenus, would be introduced into the story: the Satyrs would form the chorus. In *Cyclops*, Silenus and his satyrs have already come into contact with Polyphemus and been enslaved by him. The Satyrs were not heroic, but are always ready to join in witty repartee – from a safe distance. Silenus provides much of the humour, derived in large measure from his insatiable desire for alcohol.

Both Satyrs and Silenus have the ultimate aim of rejoining Dionysus and returning to a life of Bacchic revelry. In spite of the intrusions of Silenus and the Satyrs, the underlying story follows traditional lines and reaches its traditional conclusion.

Inscribed victory lists suggest that, around 486 BC at the Dionysia, Chionides was the first victor to present a play representative of Old Comedy. Aristophanes is the best known exponent of comedies of this type. The comedies were satirical (a word unconnected with Satyrs) and provided much greater scope for comedy than the restrictive format of the Satyr plays. Rather than mythological stories, the lampooning of politicians and any public figure worthy of attention took

9

centre-stage. However, tragedy, Old Comedy and Satyr plays seem to have co-existed through to the end of the fifth century. The Athenian defeat in the Peloponnesian War in 404 BC saw changes take place. The fourth century saw little of tragedy and few, if any, Satyr plays. There follows quite a lengthy period where little is known of comedy production; but towards the end of the fourth century, New Comedy emerged. With poets such as Menander, the chorus fell away, and drama took more the format of modern plays. Many stock characters emerged: young men in love, slaves cleverer than their masters, female slaves who turn out to be well-born, braggart soldiers, irascible old men who complain about their wives. But all this became far removed from the fifth century tragedies, Old Comedy and Satyr plays.

Odysseus and the Cyclops in Homer

The underlying mythological story upon which *Cyclops* is based can be found in Homer's *Odyssey* (*Book IX, 106 – 566*):

"We came to the land of the arrogant, lawless Cyclopes, who trust in the immortal gods and make no effort either to plant or to plough; but everything grows without sowing or ploughing – wheat, barley and the vines, rich in grapes, which bring forth wine – and the rains from Zeus make them grow. For them, there is no commerce or Councils or law courts: but they live in the hollow caves amidst the peaks of lofty mountains. Each sets the laws for his wife and children; but they have no care for each other.

Now, a fertile island lay before us outside the harbour of the Cyclopes' land, neither near nor too far off, and woody. There, countless goats live wild. For, no man-made paths keep them away, and no hunters, who might bear the rigours of the woods to frequent the mountain tops, track them. Nor is the island the home of shepherds or ploughmen, but rather, unsown and unploughed, each and every day it is devoid of men and provides pasture for bleating goats. The Cyclopes have no red-cheeked ships nor shipbuilders to produce the well-decked ships in which to cross to foreign cities to acquire those goods for which men traverse the seas to visit each other, and to make the island wealthy for themselves. The land there is not poor, and would bring forth anything in its season. By the shores of the grey sea are well-watered soft meadows in which are ample vines. There is arable land, and deep standing crops are always harvested in season, since the land is rich below the surface. There is a harbour with good mooring, where there is no need of cables or anchor-stones or making fast the sterns, but a ship can run ashore and stay until the crew is minded to move and fair winds blow. But at the head of the

11

harbour, a spring lets clear water flow from a cave. Around it grow black poplars. We sailed as far as this: some god guided us through the darkness of the night; it was impossible to see ahead. There was a heavy mist round the ships, and the moon did not shine from the heavens, but rather was covered by cloud. No-one could see the island with their eyes nor did we see the long waves rolling in on the shore before our well-decked ships had beached. Once landed, we took down all the ships' sails and we ourselves disembarked onto the sea-shore. We then fell asleep and awaited the goodly dawn.

But when there appeared the early-born rosy-fingered dawn, we were amazed at the island and roamed about it. Nymphs, the daughters of aegis-bearing Zeus, roused maintain goats in order that my comrades might dine. We immediately took supple bows and long spears from our ships, and, dividing ourselves into three groups, we let fly at the goats and a god gave us a haul of meat to our taste. Twelve ships were following me, and to each were allotted nine goats. To me alone they allotted ten. Then, all day long, until the sun set, we sat enjoying the rich meat and sweet wine. For there remained some red wine in our ships: it had not all been used up. We had sacked the holy city of the Cicones and every man had drawn off quantities of wine into jars. And so, being close by, we gazed at the land of the Cyclopes: we could see the smoke from their fires and hear the bleating of their sheep and goats.

But when the sun set and darkness came, we slept on the sea-shore.

But when there appeared the early-born rosy-fingered dawn, then I held a council with everyone and said:

'My steadfast comrades, the rest of you must wait here whilst I with my ship and its crew go to find out about these men, who they are, whether they are savage, fierce and unjust, or whether they are hospitable and respect the gods'.

Having spoken, I went aboard my ship and ordered my comrades to embark and cast off. They embarked again, sat at the benches and in turn beat the grey sea with their oars. But as we reached the nearby land, we saw a cave on the shore close by the sea. It was lofty and covered in laurel. There, there were many flocks: sheep and goats were calling out. A courtyard had been formed with lofty walls of rounded stones, tall pines and high-topped trees. A monstrous man slept in there, who, alone, tended his flocks round about. He did not go about with others, nor, living apart, did he recognize any laws. What an amazing monster he was! He was unlike any food-eating man but rather like the wooded peak of lofty mountains that appears alone away from the others.

So then, I ordered the rest of my steadfast comrades to wait by the ship and to guard it. I then chose twelve of my best men and set off. I had with me a goatskin flask of dark wine which had been given to me by Maron, the son of Euanthes, priest of Apollo, the god dwelling in Ismarus, since we had protected him and his wife and child out of reverence for him: he lived in the wooded grove of Phoebus Apollo. He gave me notable gifts: he gave me seven talents of wrought gold; he gave me a solid silver mixing bowl; and then he gave me sweet unmixed wine, a divine drink, pouring it into all of twelve jars. None of the servants or serving-girls in his house knew of the wine, which was known of by himself, his dear wife and by one housekeeper only. Whenever they had drunk of this honey-sweet red wine, they filled one goblet and added twenty parts of water: but the sweet fragrance rising from the mixing-bowl was heavenly. You would not have found it pleasant to abstain! I filled a great skin full of this wine, and also took some food in a bag. My valiant spirit had an immediate feeling that we would come upon a fierce man, endowed with great prowess, knowing neither right nor respect for the gods.

We quickly reached the cave, but did not find him inside. Instead he was tending his fat flocks in the pasture. We entered the cave and looked closely at its contents. There were baskets filled with cheeses and pens crammed with sheep and their lambs. They had been divided so that the older sheep were together, as were the later-born, and then the newly-born. All his well-made vessels – milk-pails and bowls which he used in milking – were overflowing with whey. My comrades at first begged me to seize some cheeses and then return so that we might drive kids and lambs quickly out of their pens to our swift ship and then set sail across the briny sea. But I was not persuaded, thinking it would be more valuable if I could see him and perhaps he might, out of hospitality, give me gifts. But in fact, when he appeared, he was going to be a far from welcome sight to my comrades.

Then, we lit a fire and made offerings to the gods. We took some cheese and ate it; and then we waited inside until the shepherd arrived. He carried a mighty load of dry wood to burn to accompany his dinner and he threw this down inside the cave with a crash. We were frightened and hurried away to an inner part of the cavern. Then, into the broad cave he drove his fat flocks, that is, those which he milked; the males – the rams and billy goats – he left at the doorway, outside in the steep-sided courtyard. Then he picked up a mightily heavy stone which he placed to close the cave entrance. Not even two and twenty strong four-wheeled carts could have rolled that stone away from the cave threshold, such was the massiveness of the stone he placed as a door. Sitting down, he began to milk the ewes and bleating goats, each in turn, and then he put their young to each. Half of the white milk he curdled, and, gathering it up, he placed it into wicker baskets; and half he poured into jars so that he could take hold of it and drink it to accompany his dinner. Then, having pressed on and finished his labours, he lit a fire, looked in towards us and said to us:

'Strangers, who are you? From where have you sailed across the sea's highways? Do you come on some business, or do you wander randomly over the sea like pirates that wander, risking their lives, as they bring evil to others?'

Thus he spoke; and our hearts beat loudly since we were afraid of his deep voice and because he was such a monster. But I replied to him thus with these words:

'We are Greeks who have been driven by the winds, from Troy, across the depths of the sea. We want to return home but have come here on a different path and course. Such has Zeus wanted and planned for us. Let it be known that we are of the armies of Agamemnon, son of Atreus, whose renown is now the greatest under the heavens since he sacked so great a city and destroyed its many armies. Now, we have come here, suppliants at your knees, asking that, out of hospitality, you might provide me with gifts or otherwise show your generosity. This is the law relating to strangers. And sir, respect the gods: we are your suppliants. Zeus, the god of strangers, is the avenger of suppliants and strangers: he it is that provides that strangers be respected.'

Thus I spoke; and he immediately replied with ruthless spirit:

'You are a fool, stranger, or you come from a long way off, if you tell me either to fear or to avoid the gods. The Cyclopes do not care about aegis-bearing Zeus or the blessed gods, since we are much the stronger. I would spare neither you nor your comrades in order to avoid the enmity of Zeus, unless my own heart told me to. But tell me where you moored your well-wrought ship when you came – whether on the shore or nearby. I wish to know.'

Thus he spoke; he was testing me, but he did not fool me; I understood all, and I answered straight back with these guileful words:

15

'Poseidon the Earth-shaker has just wrecked my ship on your land, driving it against the headland and hurling it onto the rocks. The wind had driven us from the ocean. But I, with these comrades, escaped the fall of death.'

Thus I spoke; but, with ruthless spirit, he replied to me nothing. Rather, he rose up and laid hands on my comrades. He seized two of them and dashed their heads on the earth as if they were puppies. Their brains ran out onto the ground and wet the earth. He tore them limb from limb and prepared them for his dinner. He ate them as would a mountain lion: he left nothing of their inwards, flesh or marrow-filled bones. We, however, when we saw these shocking deeds, wept and held up our hands to Zeus. Helplessness overwhelmed my spirit. And when the Cyclops had filled his great stomach by eating human flesh and drinking undiluted milk, he stretched out amongst his flocks inside the cave. I then deliberated with great-heartedness of spirit, thinking to get nearer to him, draw the sharp sword by my thigh and, clutching the sword in my hand, to strike him in the chest where the midriff holds the liver. But another thought prevented me; for, we also in that place would have suffered the fall of death, since we would have been unable to push back with our hands the mighty stone which he had placed in the lofty entrance. Thus, then, weeping, we awaited the goodly dawn.

But when there appeared the early-born rosy-fingered dawn, he lit a fire and milked his fine flocks, each in their turn, and he put their young to each. Then, having pressed on and finished his labours, he again seized two men together and prepared a meal. He ate and then drove his fat flocks from the cave, easily removing the heavy stone that closed the entrance. But then he replaced it, as if he were replacing the cap on a quiver. With much playing of his pipe, the Cyclops turned the fat flocks towards the mountain. But I was left, brooding darkly whether I could in some way be avenged and whether

Athene would answer my prayer. And the following seemed to my mind to be the best plan. There lay, belonging to the Cyclops, by a pen, a great club of green olive: he had cut it so that he could carry it when it had been seasoned. We thought it looked the size of a mast of a black twenty-oared ship – a broad merchantman – which sails the deep. Such was its length and thickness from its appearance. I went up to it and cut off a length about equal to my outstretched arms and passed it on to my comrades ordering them to sharpen it. They made it smooth, and then I came and brought it to a sharp point and then, taking hold of it, I hardened it in the blazing fire. Then I placed it ready, hiding it under some dung, of which there were exceedingly large amounts throughout the cave. I told the others to draw lots as to who should venture with me to lift the stake and twist it in his eye when sweet sleep overtook him. Those chosen by lot were the men I would have chosen: there were four of them and I was chosen as the fifth. In the evening, he came, shepherding his thick-fleeced flocks. Then, into the broad cave he drove his fat flocks – all of them – none was left in the steep-sided courtyard. Perhaps he suspected something; perhaps a god instructed him. Then he picked up a mightily heavy stone which he placed to close the cave entrance, and, sitting down, he began to milk the ewes and bleating goats, each in turn, and he put their young to each. Then, having pressed on and finished his labours, he again seized two men together and prepared his dinner. And then I stood beside the Cyclops and spoke to him, having in my hands an ivy-wood drinking-cup full of dark wine:
'Cyclops, come, drink some wine now that you have eaten human flesh, so that you can see what kind of drink our ship conceals. I brought some as an offering to you in the hope that you would have mercy on us and send us homeward. But you have shown a madness no longer to be borne. You shameless

creature! How could anyone from the cities of men come to visit you after this, since you do not act within your rights?' Thus I spoke. He accepted the wine and drank it. As he drank the sweet wine, he enjoyed it so enormously that he asked me for a second drink.

'Kindly give me some more; and now you must tell me your name that I might, out of hospitality, give you gifts which you will appreciate. For, the life-giving soil bears the Cyclopes vines to make wine and the rains from Zeus makes them grow; but this is a distillation of ambrosia and nectar.'

Thus he spoke; and I passed him some more of the glistening wine. Three times I brought him some more; and three times he foolishly drank. But when the wine went to the Cyclops' head, it was then that I spoke to him with gentle words:

'Cyclops, you ask me the name by which I am known. And so I will tell you; and you should then give me, out of hospitality, the gifts you promised. Nobody is my name. My mother and father call me that and so do all my comrades.'

Thus I spoke; and he immediately replied with ruthless spirit: 'Nobody I shall eat last of these comrades – the others first. That, out of hospitality, shall be your gift!'

Then, leaning backwards, he fell on his back. There he lay with his thick neck bent sideways; and all-conquering sleep came over him. Bursting out of his throat came wine and morsels of human flesh as, drunk, he vomited. And then I drove the stake well under the embers whilst they were still hot; I encouraged all my comrades with words lest any should shrink back from fear. But as soon as the olive stake in the fire was about to catch alight and glowed fiercely, I quickly took it out of the fire. My comrades gathered round me, and some god inspired them with boldness. They seized the olive stake, its end sharp, and fixed it firmly into his eye. At the same time, I pressed from underneath and twisted it round, as a man bores a ship's timber with a drill whilst men below spin it with a strap that they hold at either end, so that the drill turns continuously. Thus we took the stake with its fiery point and twisted it round in his eye; and hot blood ran down over him. The heat singed all around his eyelids and eyebrow as his eyeball burnt and the roots of his eye crackled. Just as when a blacksmith dips a great axe or adze into cold water, it makes a great roar as he tempers it, such being the power of iron, so the roots of his eye hissed around the olive stake. He gave a horrendously great cry of pain: the rocks echoed all around and we drew back in fear. From his eye, he pulled out the stake, heavily stained with blood, and then, distraught, he threw it from him; with a loud voice, he called the Cyclopes who lived in the caves round about him throughout the wooded headland. And they, hearing his shouts, came out each from a different place. They stood around his cave and asked what the matter was:

'Polyphemus, what causes you such distress that you shout so through the divinely-given night and make us lose our sleep? Surely someone is not rustling your sheep? Surely someone is not trying to kill you – by cunning or violence?'

From his cave, the mighty Polyphemus spoke to them:

'My friends, Nobody is killing me by cunning and violence!'

They in reply, spoke these winged words:

'If then there is no-one who is attacking you and you are alone, and since there is no way of fending off illness sent by great Zeus, then you must pray to your father, Lord Poseidon.'

Thus they spoke and went away; and my dear heart laughed at how my name and excellent cunning had deceived them. But the Cyclops, wailing with pain, groped with his hands and took the stone out of the doorway. He himself sat in the doorway and stretched out his arms to see if he could catch anyone trying to get to the door with his sheep. He assumed that I was so lacking in wit. But I deliberated how this could turn out best and whether I could find any escape from death for my comrades and myself. I wove every scheme and plan to save our souls: for, a great evil was at hand. And the following seemed to my mind to be the best plan. There were some rams, well-bred, thick-fleeced, of great size with purple-dark wool. Silently, with the supple twigs on which slept the monstrous Cyclops, who respected not the gods, I bound the rams together in threes: the middle ones would each carry a man whilst the pair on either side would shield the man as they went. I, however, (for there was a ram which was the best of the whole flock) seized this animal by the back and lay coiled up close to its shaggy belly, unceasingly with steadfast heart clutching with my hands the heavenly choice fleece. Thus then, lamenting, we awaited the goodly dawn.

But when there appeared the early-born rosy-fingered dawn, then the male of the flocks rushed out to pasture, but the females bleated unmilked by their pens, since their udders were bursting. Their master, worn out by great pain, felt the backs of all the sheep as they stood up near him. He foolishly did not realise that the men were tied to the undersides of the woolly sheep. The last ram of the flock began to move to the doorway burdened both by his wool and by me with my crowded thoughts. Feeling his back, the mighty Polyphemus spoke to him:

'My pet ram, why do you rush out of the cave the last of all my flocks? You have never been left behind before. You are always the first to stride out to feed on the soft flowers, the first to reach the flowing rivers, and the first to want to return to the fold in the evening. Now you are the last. Do you grieve for the eye of your master whom an evil man with his baneful comrades has blinded, having overcome my wits with wine – Nobody, who, I say, has not yet escaped death. If only you could feel as I do and acquire a voice so that you could tell me where that man is avoiding my might. Then his brains would be dashed out and would run all over the ground, and my heart

20

would be eased of the pain brought on me by that worthless Nobody.'

Having come a little way from the cave and the courtyard, I freed myself firstly from my ram and then freed my comrades. Frequently looking back, we drove the long-legged flocks, rich in fat, until we came to our ship. We that had escaped death were a welcome sight to our dear comrades, but for the others they began to weep and lament. But I would not allow such weeping and indicated the fact to each with a nod and a raised eyebrow. Rather, I ordered them quickly to drive the thick-fleeced flocks onto the ship and then set sail across the briny sea. They embarked again, sat at the benches and in turn beat the grey sea with their oars. And when we were as far away as a man can shout, then I spoke to the Cyclops with this reproach:

'Cyclops, you are not going to eat the comrades of some cowardly man in your hollow cave for all your might and violence. Rather, your evil deeds will seek you out, you shameless creature, since you did not baulk at eating strangers in your home. Zeus and the other gods have wrought vengeance on you.'

Thus I spoke, but he then became angrier in his heart. He tore off the top of a great mountain peak and threw it down a little in front of our blue-prowed ship, falling short of our lofty helm. The sea was forced up by the falling rock; and the backward force of the wave, a flood from the ocean, bore the ship back towards the shore, so that we were headed towards the beach. I seized a long pole in my hands and pushed us back out. I encouraged my comrades, telling them with nods of my head to push off with their oars so that we might escape the danger. They rushed to drive us forwards. When we were twice as far away across the sea, then I began to speak to the Cyclops, but all around me my comrades restrained me with these gentle words:

'You shameless creature, why do you want to anger a wild man who has already made an assault on our ship which was headed for the ocean and driven it back to the shore: we were sure we were going to die there and then. If he had heard anyone speak or make a noise, he would have smashed our heads and our ship's timbers to pieces with the strike of a jagged piece of sparkly rock. He can throw as far as this.'

Thus they spoke; but they did not persuade my great-hearted spirit. And I spoke to him once more with anger:

'Cyclops, if some mortal man asks you about the shameful blinding of your eye, say that Odysseus, sacker of cities, son of Laërtes, who has his home in Ithaca, blinded you!'

Thus I spoke; and he, groaning, replied to me with these words:

'Ah! So then indeed, an ancient prophecy has come true. A fine and great man, a seer, Telemus son of Eurymus, was once here, who was skilled in divination, and as a seer, grew old amongst the Cyclopes. He told me that all this would happen – that I would lose my sight at the hands of Odysseus. But I always expected that some great, well-made man would come here, clothed in great prowess. But now someone small, worthless and feeble has blinded my eye, after he had overcome me with wine. But come back, Odysseus, so that I might, out of hospitality, give you gifts and urge the noble Earthshaker to provide an escort. For, I am his son and he claims to be my father; and he, if he wants to, will heal me – which none other of the blessed gods or mortal men will do.'

Thus he spoke; but I spoke to him in reply:

'If only I could separate you from your soul and life, so as to send you to the house of Hades, with as much certainty as I have that not even the Earthshaker will heal your eye.'

Thus I spoke; and then he prayed to Lord Poseidon, raising up his hands to the starry heavens:

'Hear me, black-haired Poseidon, girdler of the Earth! If I am truly yours and you claim to be my father, grant my wish that this man does not reach his home – Odysseus, sacker of cities, son of Laërtes, who has his home in Ithaca. But if it is his fate to see his loved ones and reach his well-built home and native land, may he arrive late and in poor state, having lost all his comrades, in a foreign ship, and may he find troubles there.'

Thus he spoke in prayer; and the black-haired one heard him. Then he immediately picked up a much greater stone and sent it spinning towards us. He put all his strength into the throw, and it came down a little behind our blue-prowed ship, falling short of our lofty helm. The sea was forced up by the falling rock and the backward force of the wave, a flood from the ocean, bore the ship back towards the shore, so that we were headed towards the beach.

But when we came to the island, where the other well-decked ships remained together, and our comrades were sitting, grieving, and waiting for us the whole time, we came and beached our ship on the sand and we ourselves disembarked onto the sea-shore. We drove the flocks of the Cyclops from the hollow ship and divided them out such that no-one was cheated of an equal share. When they divided up the flocks, my comrades allocated the ram especially to me alone. On the shore, to Zeus, the black-clouded son of Cronos, I sacrificed him and burnt his limbs: but Zeus did not heed my offering, but rather planned how all my well-decked ships and faithful comrades might be lost.

Then, all day long, until the sun set, we sat enjoying the rich meat and sweet wine. But when the sun set and darkness came, we slept on the sea-shore.

But when there appeared the early-born rosy-fingered dawn, I encouraged my comrades and ordered them to embark and cast off. They embarked again, sat at the benches and in turn beat the grey sea with their oars.

Then we sailed on with grief in our hearts, pleased to escape death, but having lost our dear comrades."

Mythological references in *Cyclops*

The Satyrs and Silenus are devotees of Dionysus and there are several references in *Cyclops* to mythological stories about him:

Dionysus, Hera and the Nymphs

SILENUS "First of all, you were driven mad by Hera and you left the mountain Nymphs, your nurses, and went away;" (*line 3*)

The story of the birth of Dionysus, his being raised by the Nymphs, the jealousy of Hera, her driving Dionysus mad and Dionysus' wanderings is set out by Apollodorus (or attributed to Apollodorus, probably 1st or 2nd century AD):

"Born to Cadmus were daughters Autonoë, Ino, Semele and Agauë and a son Polydorus. Athamas married Ino, Aristaeus married Autonoë and Echion married Agauë. Zeus was attracted to Semele and slept with her unbeknown to Hera. Deceived by Hera, and promised by Zeus that he would grant her any wish, she asked that he would come to her as he did when he courted Hera. Zeus, being unable to refuse came to her chamber on a chariot with thunder and lightning and launched a thunderbolt. Semele died of fright; but Zeus snatched up their six-month abortive child from the fire and sewed it into his thigh. After Semele's death, the remaining daughters of Cadmus spread the word that Semele had slept with some mortal man but that she had blamed Zeus, and because of this, she had been struck by his thunderbolt. But when the time came, Zeus bore Dionysus by undoing the sewing, and gave him to Hermes. Hermes took him to Ino and Athamas and persuaded them to bring him up as a girl. Hera

25

was angered and drove them mad….. Zeus, by changing Dionysus into a kid, evaded the anger of Hera; and Hermes, taking him, conveyed him to the Nymphs living in Nysa in Asia, whom Zeus later changed into stars and called them the Hyades." (*Apollodorus, Bibliotheca III iv 3*)

"Dionysus, became the discoverer of the vine. When Hera had driven him mad, he wandered about Egypt and Syria." (*Apollodorus, Bibliotheca III v 1*)

Dionysus' being raised by the Nymphs is described in Homeric *Hymns* (7th to 4th century BC):

"My song of Dionysus, ivy-crowned,
begin – of glorious Semele and Zeus
the famous son – whom rich-haired nymphs once nursed,
received to their breasts from his father, tended with care
in the vales of Nysa. Raised at his father's will
in a fragrant cave, amongst the gods was he named.
But when the nymphs had raised their much-hymned charge,
began he wanderings wide through wooded dales,
bedecked with bay and ivy. Nymphs in train
he led; and revelry filled the boundless woods.
        So hail o Dionysus god of wine!
        That we rejoice this season grant again,
        and from this season, on for years to come."
(*Homeric Hymn XXVI, To Dionysus*)

"At Drakanon or windy Ikaros
or Naxos, goodly Bacchus, as some say,
or by th'eddying river Alpheios,
there, Semele bore you, to Zeus the King,
whilst others, Lord, say you were born in Thebes.
They lie. The father of men and gods bore you,

26

abroad, unknown to white-armed Hera, thus:
There is a wooded mountain, Nysa, high
beyond Phoenicia, near Egyptian streams ...."
(*Fragment: Homeric Hymn I, To Bacchus*)

The Battle of the Giants (Gigantomachia): The parts played by Dionysus and Silenus; the death of Enceladus

SILENUS "...then later, there was that battle with the Earthborn, when I stood, a comrade-in-arms, at your right hand, and I drove my spear through the middle of Enceladus' shield and killed him."
(*lines 5 – 8*)

The story of the Giants' battle against the gods is recounted by Nonnus in his epic poem Dionysiaca (probably 5th or 4th century BC). The Giants were born of Gaia, Mother Earth, and are hence also known as the 'Earthborn'. Silenus' role in the battle is not mentioned in this passage by Nonnus, who suggests that Enceladus, far from being killed by Silenus, was later killed by Zeus' thunderbolt.

"Bacchus, riding his chariot pulled by leopards, passed over the Thracian land in revelry, having left the horsebreeding land of the ancient family of Phoroneus (*son of Inachus, ruler of Argos*). But Hera, friend of Inachus, did not cease in her old anger concerning Argos which had been stung into madness. She retained a memory of the frenzy of the Achaean women there, and again prepared arms against Bacchus. She made deceitful prayers to Gaia, the All-Mother Earth. She complained of the deeds of Zeus and the prowess of Dionysus, who had destroyed a cloud of countless earthborn men of the Indus. And when the life-giving Mother Earth heard that the

27

child of Semele had destroyed the race of the doomed men of the Indus, thinking of her children, she wailed all the more. Then, against Bacchus, she armed her own-born mountain-ranging race of the Giants and goaded her own high-crested sons to battle-glory:

'My children, attack the garlanded Dionysus with massive rocks. Come against this Indian-killing slaughterer of my race, the son of Zeus; never shall I see this bastard son bearing a sceptre and ruling with Zeus over Olympus. Bind, bind Bacchus, so that he may act as my servant when I give my daughters in marriage to Giants, Hebe to Porphyrion and Cytheria to Chthonius, and when I sing of the grey-eyed mistress of Enceladus and of Artemis mistress of Alcyoneus. Bring me Dionysus that I may anger the son of Cronos when he sees the slavery of his spear-bearing Deliverer. Or strike him with your deadly iron swords. Kill him for me like Zagreus, so that god and servant may say that Gaia, in anger at the race of the sons of Cronos has twice armed her avengers – the older Titans against the younger Dionysus, and the younger Giants against the later-born Dionysus.'

Having spoken thus, she roused the whole army of the Giants, and the ranks of the Earthborn marched forth for battle-glory: one holding a massive piece of Mount Nysa, another cutting off a cloud-high mountain gully; each armed with rocks as these, they advanced against Dionysus. One carried a rocky hill which had reached down to the sea, another held a ridge torn from a sea-girt isthmus. Each hurried to the battle. Peloreus took lofty-peaked Pelion as weapons for his countless arms, laying bare the cave-home of Philyra: and, as the roof of his cave was snatched away, old Chiron trembled – part man, part comrade horse. But Bacchus, holding a cluster of grapes, deadly to Giants, charged at lofty-crested Alcyoneus. He had no stout spear; he wielded no bloody sword; but he tore off the sprouting arms of the Giants, by

28

thrusting with the fruits of the vine. Masses of bristling ground-reared snakes were cut down by the wine-beloved leaves. As the Giant snake-haired heads were cut off, the severed necks began to dance in the dust. Countless masses were killed. As the Giants were slaughtered, there flowed unending rivers of blood, and the gullies ran red with new-flowing streams of crimson. The ranks of the earthborn snakes fell to frenzy before the locks of snake-haired Dionysus.

And Bacchus waged war with fire. He hurled a torch into the air, bringing death to his enemies. The curling, leaping flame of Bacchus ran along the upper paths, rushing down on the Giants with limb-devouring sparks. And some half-burnt snake, with flame in his threatening jaws, whistled from its fire-ravaged throat, spitting out smoke instead of hurling its poisonous dart.

The battle-din was indescribable. Bacchus raised his battle-torch over the heads of his enemies and scorched the bodies of the Giants with an earthly hurricane-lightening, a resounding image of Zeus' thunderbolt. Torches blazed. Wandering brands made the air hot and quivered around the head of Enceladus. But they did not kill him: Enceladus did not bend his knee to the vapours of earthly fire since he was saved – for a thunderbolt.

Mighty Alcyoneus leapt on Bacchus, armed with Thracian rocks. Over him, he raised the cloud-high snow-covered peak of Mount Haimos, but with useless aim, since Dionysus was invulnerable. He threw his hill-top, but when this summit touched Bacchus' untearable fawnskin, it split in pieces itself. Lofty Typhöeus had stripped the head of Mount Emathia – he was like his predecessor, who often tore up the ragged hollows of his Mother Earth – and launched at Dionysus with his rocky missiles. But Lord Bacchus took up the sword of one who was gasping on the ground and swung at the Giants' heads, cutting off the snake-writhing mass of dart-shooting hair. Cutting

29

down the spontaneous army with his weaponless hand, he battled with rage, holding long-leafed tree-climbing ivy branches to spear the Giants.

Now, he would have slain them all with his rank-breaking wand, had not he, who had turned to fight again and again, retired from the fray, keeping many enemies alive – for his father."

(*Nonnos, Dionysiaca XLVIII 1 – 89*)

Hyginus (1st century AD), quoting Eratosthenes, depicts a lesser role for Dionysus, and also for the Sileni in general.

"There is another story told about the Asses (*two stars in the Crab constellation*). As Eratosthenes says: at that time when Jupiter had declared war on the Giants, he called together all the gods to oppose them and the father Liber (*Dionysus*), Vulcan, the Satyrs and Sileni came on asses, which, since they were not far from the enemy, were said to become frightened and each one raised a great braying unheard before by the Giants, so that all the enemies turned to flight at their noise and so were overcome." (*Hyginus, Astronomica II 23*)

Enceladus' particular relevance to *Cyclops* lies in the ancient tradition that volcanos erupted because there were Giants buried beneath them, who every now and again turned over and caused an eruption. Enceladus was traditionally the Giant buried under Mount Etna, as depicted by Virgil (1st century BC):

"The harbour itself is calm, being free from the winds, and huge. But close by, Etna thunders with horrific ruination. Often, it throws a black cloud to the sky, fuming with a pitchy storm of falling ash. It raises up balls of flame and licks the stars. Sometimes it vomits and hurls up rocks, the torn entrails of the mountain. With a groan, it solidifies the molten rocks under the breezes and boils over from its lower depths. The story is that the body of Enceladus, half-burnt by a thunderbolt is under the weight of this mass and that massive Etna, deposited above him, breathes out flame from its ruptured furnaces; and that as often as he turns over on his side, tired, the whole of Trinacrian Sicily quakes with a murmur and covers the sky with smoke." (*Virgil, Aeneid III 570 – 582*)

There is a further tradition that Enceladus was not killed by Zeus' thunderbolt, but by Athene:

"And Athene threw the island of Sicily on the fleeing Enceladus." (*Apollodorus, Bibliotheca, I vi 2*)

Dionysus snatched by Tyrrhenian pirates

SILENUS "For, Hera has had a band of Tyrrhenian pirates seize you, and you are now a long way off about to be sold into slavery;"
(*lines 11 – 12*)

An account of the attempt by Tyrrhenian pirates to kidnap Dionysus is told in a Homeric *Hymn*:

"How Dionysus, son of Semele,
appeared in the form of a man in the bloom of youth,
on a headland high by the shore of the fruitless sea,
I'll tell. His rich dark hair about him waved;
he wore on shoulders strong a purple cloak.
But fast there came in sight with a well-decked ship
on the wine-dark sea, Tyrrhenian pirates swift;
an evil fate them led. They looked and saw

31

and nodded each. Ashore they ran and him
they seized; then sailed away with gladdened hearts
and said 'The son of well-born kings is he'.
They tried to bind him fast with painful bonds;
but bonds restrained him not. The fastenings fell
away from hands and feet. He sat and smiled,
with dark blue eyes. And when the helmsman saw,
he shouted to his comrades words as these:
'My friends, what god is this we've seized and bound?
He's strong. Our well-made ship him cannot hold.
For, he is Zeus, Apollo silver-bowed,
or else Poseidon, seeming not to be
of mortal men but of th' Olympian gods!
But let us set him free on the black sea-shore
straightway, nor lay our hands on him, lest he
in anger raise up winds and furious storms.'
The captain answered him with these harsh words:
'My friend, *you* watch the wind and raise the sail:
take hold the sheets. And *men* will see to him!
To Egypt will he come or Cyprus, or
to th' Hyperboreans or further still.
By then he'll name his friends and brothers, tell
of all his riches: for, he's ours from god.'
He spoke, and had the mast and sail raised up.
A wind blew up and filled the sail; they hauled
the sheets full taut. But then, strange happenings:
Throughout the swift black ship there bubbled wine,
so sweet to drink, ambrosial in its scent.
Astounded were the crew who stood and watched:
Along the sail, on high, a vine spread out
from side to side, on which there heavy hung
abundant grapes, and round the mast there grew
an ivy full of flower and beauteous fruit.
The oar-pins all were garlanded; and they

that saw the ship then urged the helmsman straight
to go to land. Their captive then became
a lion, fearsome, high upon the ship.
He roared, and in their midst a shaggy bear
he set, by hunger roused; from th' upper deck
the lion glared. The crew all fled astern
and round the helmsman, (wise and steadfast he),
they crowded fearful. Rose the lion quick,
and seized the captain. Seeing this, the crew
leapt off the ship to escape their fate in the sea:
but dolphins they became. The helmsman, though,
he pitied, held him back, and blessed him thus:
'Take courage, helmsman pleasing to my heart!
For, Dionysus, born of Semele
the Cadmeïd, am I; my father, Zeus.'
      So hail, the child of fair-eyed Semele!
      No song could I arrange forgetting you."
(*Homeric Hymn VII, To Dionysus*)

Maron's wine

ODYSSEUS "Yes, and Maron, the son of a god, gave me
    the drink."
SILENUS "Maron! But I raised him in these arms of
    mine!.."
ODYSSEUS "...the son of Dionysus, as you clearly know
    better than I."
(*lines 141 – 123*)

For Silenus, as before, truth is no obstacle: he speaks for
    effect.

In Homer, Maron is "Maron, the son of Euanthes, priest of Apollo, the god dwelling in Ismarus, …: he lived in the wooded grove of Phoebus Apollo". (*Odyssey IX, 197 – 201*)

The stage setting for Cyclops

Homer describes the Cyclops' cave with a courtyard in front of it:

"…we saw a cave on the shore close by the sea. It was lofty and covered in laurel. …A courtyard had been formed with lofty walls of rounded stones, tall pines and high-topped trees." (*Odyssey IX, 181 – 186*)

"We entered the cave and looked closely its contents. There were baskets filled with cheeses and pens crammed with sheep and their lambs. …. All his well-made vessels – milk-pails and bowls which he used in milking – were overflowing with whey." (*Odyssey IX, 218 – 223*)

"Then, into the broad cave he drove his fat flocks, that is, those which he milked; the males – the rams and billy goats – he left at the doorway, outside in the steep-sided courtyard. Then he picked up a mightily heavy stone which he placed to close the cave entrance. Not even two and twenty strong four-wheeled carts could have rolled that stone away from the cave threshold, such was the massiveness of the stone he placed as a door. Sitting down, he began to milk the ewes and bleating goats, each in turn, and then he put their young to each. … Then, having pressed on and finished his labours, he lit a fire, looked in towards us…"
(*Odyssey IX, 237 – 251*)

Homer then envisages a cave close to the sea. Its entrance is surrounded by a high-walled courtyard. The pens for the sheep and goats, together with all the milking equipment, are contained inside the cave. The Cyclops milks his sheep and goats inside the cave, having first closed the entrance with a huge stone. When milking is finished, he lights a fire in the cave. The male animals, however, may be left overnight in the courtyard.

Euripides follows later tradition and places the cave by the sea at the foot of Mount Etna in Sicily.

The stage for *Cyclops* is set outside Polyphemus' cave. There is an entrance from the stage into the cave, and this entrance has a door: "Listen now! The Cyclops calls out 'Who will open me the door now?' " (*line 502*).
There is a view down to the sea, and, in particular, to Odysseus' ship. "I can see a Greek ship at the headland. And the captain and his crew are walking up towards this cave." (*lines 85 – 87*)
The courtyard depicted by Homer is absent. The ground is "lush and full of flowers" (*line 541*). Outside the cave, therefore, are the lower pastures, and the sheep and at least some of the sheep-pens are close at hand but offstage. The First Choral Song (*lines 41 – 81*) can certainly be played in such a way that the audience feels that it is taking the part of the sheep.
This, overall, is the picture painted by the First Choral Song, and the Cyclops' question "Who's that I see by the sheep pens?" (*line 222*).

Homer has Polyphemus' sheep and goats sleeping inside the cave itself, with the male animals perhaps left in the courtyard. In *Cyclops*, the animals are never seen onstage, (in fact in *Cyclops* there are only oblique references to goats, but Polyphemus does milk his cows and drink cows' milk) and the escape by Odysseus and his men involving clinging on to the undersides of rams is dispensed with: the situation of the sheep is therefore not critical to the plot.

However, Silenus' instruction "Tell everyone to gather the flocks together inside the caves" (*line 82*) suggests that the sheep do enter the cave at some point and Odysseus is clearly speaking to animals inside the cave when he says "Quiet now, by the gods! You animals, keep calm" *(line 624)*.

The action of the play starts in the evening, the time when the sheep return from their pastures, and it is sufficiently light for Silenus to see Odysseus' ship.
But, it is dark by the time the Cyclops comes home. He needs a light to see what he is doing: "Bring a light here! Hold it up!" (*line 203*), and later the Chorus say "I myself am looking at the stars and Orion" (*lines 212 – 213*). In view of the Cyclops' order to bring a light, the Satyrs, at some time after their arrival, will have lit torches or lanterns to light the cave entrance in the growing dark.
The Cyclops drinks and sings all night. When Odysseus emerges from the cave for the Second Episode, it is already late morning and the sun is hot: Silenus is able to say: "And it's lovely drinking in the warmth of the sun. Lie on the ground next to me" (*lines 542 – 543*).

Origins and Life of Euripides

[A translation of the text of the 'Origins and Life of Euripides' is set out below. The original was transmitted along with the texts of Euripides plays, but its own origin is not known. It does not constitute a single account: sections Ia and III are considered to derive from related sources, section Ib appears to stand alone and repeats some of what is in Ia and III, and II and IV have elements from a different source.]

Ia. Euripides the poet was born the son of Mnesarchides[1], a shopkeeper, and Cleito a vegetable seller. He was an Athenian, born in Salamis, in the archonship of Calliades in the year of the 75th Olympiad[2], at the time of the Greek sea-battle against the Persians[3].

He trained, to begin with, for the pankration[4] or boxing, since his father had received an oracle that he would be victorious in contests where the winner is crowned. They say he did win a victory at Athens.

[1] In some sources referred to as Mnesarchus.

[2] 480BC.

[3] The battle of Salamis, as referred to below.

[4] Pancration: a combined form of wrestling and boxing.

Having studied, he turned to tragedy and introduced many innovations[1]: enquiries into natural causes, rhetorical speeches and recognitions, as would be expected of one who was a pupil of Anaxagoras, Prodicus and Protagoras and was a friend of Socrates.

Both the philosopher Socrates and Mnesilochus seemed to have collaborated with him: as Telecleides says: "Mnesilochus proposes some fresh Phrygian drama for Euripides and so does Socrates." [2] Others say Cephisophon or the Argive Timocrates composed songs for him.

They say that he became a painter and that he showed his paintings in Megara; and that he became a torch-bearer of Apollo Zosterius; and that he was born on the same day as Hellanicus[3] on which the Greeks were victorious at the sea-battle of Salamis; and that he first entered the drama competitions when he was 26 years old.

He settled in Magnesia[4] and was honoured with privileges[5] and freedom from taxes.

[1] Different readings of the texts suggest an additional innovation may have been 'prologues'.

[2] Again, different readings of the text (reading φρύγει τι and τὰ φρύγαν᾽ for Φρυγικὸν, may suggest the rather more colourful reading: 'Mnesilochus roasts some fresh drama for Euripides as Socrates lays the firewood'.

[3] Hellanicus of Mytilene, a lexicographer.

[4] Magnesia: in the region of Thessalia in Northern Greece.

[5] The privileges related to 'proxenia', a legal status of friendship offered to a foreigner.

From there he went to Macedonia to Archelaüs[1] and spent time there and pleased the king by writing a play bearing his name. He gained success there and was placed in charge of financial administration.

He is said to have grown a long beard and to have had moles around his eyes; and to have married firstly Melito and secondly Choerile and to have left three sons, the eldest Mnesarchides, a merchant, next Mnesilochus an actor, and the youngest Euripides who produced some of his father's plays. He began to produce plays in the archonship of Callias in the first year after the 81st Olympiad[2]. His first play was *Peliades*[3] when he also won third prize. In all he wrote 92 plays of which 78 are extant. Of these, three are spurious: Tennes, Rhadamanthys and Peirithous.

He died, according to Philochorus, when over 70 years old, and according to Eratosthenes, aged 75. He was buried in Macedonia. A cenotaph was raised to him in Athens and there was an inscription on it written either by the historian Thucydides or the songwriter Timotheus: "All Greece is a memorial of Euripides. His bones/ are in the land of Macedonia; for there he came to the end of his life./ His homeland was Athens, the Greece of Greece. Most of all, the Muses/ he pleased and receives praise from many." They say both memorials were struck by lightning.

[1] Archelaüs, King of Macedonia.

[2] 455 BC.

[3] *Peliades* or *Daughters of Pelias*.

They say that Sophocles, hearing that he had died, went out in a grey or purple cloak and that he had his chorus and actors enter the ceremonial parade without garlands and that the people wept.

III. They say that he kitted out a cave on Salamis with its entrance facing out to sea, and there he spent his days, fleeing the crowds. Hence, he took most of his analogies from the sea. He appeared to be sullen, grave and crabby as well as laughter-hating and misogynistic. This led Aristophanes to condemn him: "Euripides seems to me to be sour to talk to". They say he married Choerile, the daughter of Mnesilochus and having perceived how disreputable she was, he firstly wrote the play *Hippolytus* in which he displayed, as in triumph, the shamelessness of women, and then he divorced her. Her second husband said "She acts properly for me", to which Euripides replied, "You are an unfortunate man if you think that the same wife acts properly for one husband but not for another"; they say that he married a second wife whom he found to be more disreputable than the first and so became even bolder in his defamation of women. Women wanted to kill him, going into the cave where he continued to write.
Jealous allegations were made that Cephisophon co-wrote his tragedies.
Hermippus says that after the death of Euripides, Dionysus the tyrant of Sicily sent a talent to his heirs for him to take his harp, writing tablet and stylus, and that when he saw them, he ordered those who brought them to hang them in the shrine of the Muses, inscribing them with his and Euripides' names. For this reason Euripides was called 'most loved by foreigners' since he was loved most especially by foreigners. The Athenians were jealous of him. When a rather uneducated youth out of envy said he had bad breath, "Now, now," he said "my mouth is sweeter than honey and the Sirens."

41

Ib. Euripides, the son of Mnesarchides, an Athenian: the comic poets mocked him as the son of a vegetable seller. They say that to begin with he was a painter, but having studied under Archelaüs, the natural scientist, and Anaxagoras, he moved towards writing tragedies. Being of a rather haughty disposition, he naturally shunned the populace and was unconcerned about popularity in the theatre. As a result, this caused him harm, but helped Sophocles in equal measure. The comic poets attacked him and, out of envy, tore him to pieces. Disdaining all this, he left for Macedonia – to King Archelaüs, where, returning rather late one evening he was killed by the king's dogs. He began to produce plays in the year of the 81st Olympiad[1] in the archonship of Callias. Employing a moderately formal style, he excelled in expressiveness, setting out sharply both sides of an argument. He was unequalled in his lyrical writing, surpassing almost all lyric poets. But in his dialogues he was awkward and burdensome and in his prologues irksome. He was particularly rhetorical in the setting out of arguments, with embroidered language, and ready to refute what had already been said.

He wrote 92 plays in all of which 67 are extant; there are a further three of disputed authorship. Eight are satyr plays of which one is of disputed authorship[2]. He won five victories.

---

[1] Ie. the first year after eighty-first Olympiad, 455 BC, as reported above in Ia.

[2] This section appears to say that there were 95 plays in total of which three were of disputed authorship. 67 of the undisputed plays were extant. Of the 95 plays, eight were satyr plays (of which one was of disputed authorship). This does not accord with Ia above which states there were 92 plays in all of which three were of disputed authorship; it further states that 78 were extant.

II. He died in the following way: In Macedonia is a village called Thracon on account of Thracians once settling there. A Molossian hound of Archelaüs entered the village and wandered about. The Thracians, as was their custom, slaughtered and ate it. Archelaüs fined them a talent. Since they did not have that sum, they asked Euripides to seek a release from their debt to the king. A little later, when Euripides was walking in a certain grove outside the city, and Archelaüs came past hunting, the huntsmen set their dogs free and these attacked Euripides, and the poet was torn apart and eaten. The dogs were the offspring of the dog taken by the Thracians, whence the Macedonian saying of "dog's justice".

IV. He mocked women in his plays on account of the following: He had a homebred slave called Cephisophon, with whom he accused his own wife of behaving disreputably. To begin with he succeeded in discouraging her. But since he could not persuade her, he left his wife to him, and Cephisophon wanted to have her. Aristophanes said: "Best and blackest Cephisophon/ you sit alongside Euripides in most things/ and you co-write his songs." They say that women, on account of his criticisms which he made of them in his writings, attacked him at the Thesmophoria[1] and wanted to do away with him. But they spared him firstly because of the Muses and secondly because he promised not to speak ill of them ever again. And in *Melanippe*, he says this of them: "A criticism made by men of women/ twangs an empty bow and is a poor speech./ They are better than men, so I say."

---

[1] Thesmophoria: a festival associated with the sowing or harvesting of the crops. It honoured Demeter and Persephone. The participants were limited to adult women.

Philemon so loved him that he dared to say about his death: "If the dead in truth/ have perception as some men say/ I would hang myself so as to see Euripides."

Structure of *Cyclops*

	Lines			Page
Prologue	*1*	-	*40*	53
Entrance of the Chorus			*41*	55
First choral song	*41*	-	*81*	55
First episode	*82*	-	*355*	57
Second choral song	*356*	-	*374*	67
Second episode	*375*	-	*655*	68
Recitative	*(483*	-	*518)*	71
Recitative	*(608*	-	*623)*	77
Conclusion	*656*	-	*709*	79
Chant	*(656*	-	*662)*	79

Cyclops

('The Setting of Cyclops' and Dramatis Personae set out on pages 49 and 51 derive from the transmitted editions of the play.)

The setting of *Cyclops*

Odysseus, returning from Troy, was cast on to Sicily, where lived Polyphemus. Finding there enslaved Satyrs, in exchange for wine, he was about to take some lambs and milk from them. But Polyphemus appears and asks the reason for the men's journey. Silenus says the foreigner is a pirate and is seizing....

Dramatis Personae [1]

Silenus

Chorus

Odysseus

Cyclops

[1] Silenus, leader and 'father' of the Satyrs and devotee of the god Dionysos; Chorus of Satyrs, devotees of the god Dionysos; Odysseus, King of Ithaca and the Kephallenians; Cyclops, Polyphemus, a one-eyed giant;
Non-speaking parts: Crew of Odysseus.

Cyclops

Scene: Outside the cave of Polyphemus.

Time: The action commences one evening.

PROLOGUE

(*Enter* Silenus *from the cave*)

SILENUS Dionysus! Because of you, my troubles are legion
– and just as much now as when, in my youth, my body
was in good condition! First of all, you were driven
mad by Hera and you left the mountain Nymphs, your
nurses, and went away; then later, there was that battle
with the Earthborn, when I stood, a comrade-in-arms,
at your right hand, and I drove my spear through the
middle of Enceladus' shield and killed him.
(*Aside, in answer to a mock question from the
audience, knowing that he did not kill Enceladus and
that the part he played in the Battle of the Giants was,
at best, to sit on an ass*)
What's that? "In my dreams" did you say? By
Zeus! I showed his armour to Dionysus
himself!
But now I bear an even greater burden.
For, Hera has had a band of Tyrrhenian pirates seize
you, and you are now a long way off, about to be sold
into slavery; and when I heard about this, I set sail with
my children in search of you. In the lofty prow, I
myself handled the tiller, whilst the children sat at the
oars and made the grey sea white with their blades, as

they searched for you, my lord. We had already sailed as far as Malea, when an east wind struck us like a spear and drove us on to the rocks of Etna, where the one-eyed man-killing Cyclopes, sons of the sea-god, live in desolate caves. We were captured by one of them and are now his slaves. Our master lives here and is called Polyphemus.

Instead of enjoying Bacchic revelry, we now shepherd the flocks of this unholy Cyclops; or rather, my children shepherd his flocks in the far reaches of the hillsides – the young caring for the young. I, on the other hand, am ordered to remain here to fill the water-troughs and clean this place out – and to act as menial servant at the unholy meals of this disgusting Cyclops. Anyway, as instructed, I must clear this place with this iron rake so that we can receive my master and his flocks with a clean cave.

I can already see the children driving the flocks home. (*The sound of music and dance is heard.*) What's this? Surely your Satyric dances are not the same to you now as when you used to dance joyfully to the sound of the lyre all the way to the palace of Althaea?

ENTRANCE OF THE CHORUS

(Enter Chorus of Satyrs. *They sing to the sheep, which they are shepherding on to the lower pasture outside and into their overnight pens.)*

FIRST CHORAL SONG

[41]
CHORUS   *[strophe]*
    Child of noble line of sires
    and noble line of dams,
    why do you long for the headland's height?
    The cooling breeze blows here.
    Out of the gale is fodder lush;
    and water trickles past.
    Troughs are full at hand, and here
    your lambs for you do bleat.
                     [mesode]
    No, no, not there!
    Will you not browse where the grass is sweet?
    Oi there, I'll throw a stone at you!
    And move over here, over here, horn'd sheep,
    to the sheep pens safe
    of the Cyclops wild.
                   [antistrophe]
    Open up your udders full!
    And give your teats to your lambs.
    Them you left to rest in the pens
    asleep all day. Now see:
    bleating, they all want you now
    as into the fold you go:
    you've left the pastures green for home
    on Etna's headland steep.

All this is not Dionysus, nor
his dances, vine-leaved wand,
the noisy beating of the drum,
the glistening drops of wine
by springs of water running free.
Nor do we sing in Nysa now
your mystic "Iacchos, Iacchos" cry,
nor dance with Nymphs in search
of Aphrodite whom we chase
in white-shoe'd Bacchic dance.
O dearest, dearest Bacchus, Oh!
where have you gone, alone,
to bind your flowing auburn locks,
whilst I, your devotee,
the one-eyed Cyclops serve,
a wandering slave
in goatskin tunic black,
your friendship lost?

FIRST EPISODE

[82]

SILENUS   Quiet now! Tell everyone to gather the flocks
    together inside the caves.

CHORUS   Come on then! But what's the hurry, father?

SILENUS   I can see a Greek ship at the headland. And the
    captain and his crew are walking up towards our cave.
    There are empty bowls slung about their necks: they
    clearly need food; and they have water-pitchers.
    Poor strangers!
    Who are they? Don't they know Polyphemus and what
    he is? ...or their misfortune in coming to an
    inhospitable land and the man-eating jaw of a
    Cyclops?
    But be quiet now, so that we can learn where they've
    come from to this neighbourhood of Sicilian Etna.

(*Enter* Odysseus *with* Crew)

ODYSSEUS   Strangers, could you tell me where there are
    mountain springs to quench our thirst? And is anyone
    willing to sell me some food for my needy crew?
    What's this? It seems I've come to a city of Dionysus:
    I see a group of Satyrs by this cave.
    Greetings! I address myself firstly to the eldest of you.

SILENUS   Greetings, stranger! Please tell us who you are and
    your country.

ODYSSEUS   I am Odysseus from Ithaca, King of the
    Kephallenians.

SILENUS   I know the man, a shrewd talker, descended from
    Sisyphus.

ODYSSEUS   I am he; but don't blame me for that!

SILENUS   Where have you sailed from to land in Sicily?

ODYSSEUS From Troy, after the war there.

SILENUS Why? Don't you know your way home?

ODYSSEUS Stormy winds have driven me here.

SILENUS Oh dear; you're watched over by the same god as I.

ODYSSEUS So you were forced here as well?

SILENUS I was chasing after pirates who had snatched Dionysus.

ODYSSEUS So what place is this and who lives here?

SILENUS This is Mount Etna, the highest part of Sicily.

ODYSSEUS Where are the city walls and towers?

SILENUS There are none. These headlands are uninhabited by men.

ODYSSEUS So who owns the land? Wild beasts perhaps?

SILENUS The Cyclopes. They live in caves, not roofed houses.

ODYSSEUS And who rules them? Or is there some form of democracy?

SILENUS The Cyclopes are units; and nobody listens to nothing from no-one!

ODYSSEUS Do they sow …corn, perhaps; or what do they live on?

SILENUS They live on milk, cheese and mutton.

ODYSSEUS And the drink of Dionysus – presumably they have the grape?

SILENUS Not at all! There's no singing and dancing here!

ODYSSEUS Are they hospitable and respectful of strangers?

SILENUS They say the sweetest meat is that of strangers.

ODYSSEUS What do you mean? They enjoy killing and eating humans?

SILENUS No-one comes here who is not slaughtered.

ODYSSEUS Where is this Cyclops? Is he away from home?

SILENUS He's away. He's hunting wild animals with his dogs around Etna.

ODYSSEUS Do you know what's to be done to avoid this place?

SILENUS No, Odysseus. We'd have done it, had we known.

ODYSSEUS Sell us then the corn we need.

SILENUS There is none. As I said, there's only meat...

ODYSSEUS Well, that's a pleasant remedy for hunger.

SILENUS ...and cheese and milk.

ODYSSEUS Bring them out. I need to see them.

SILENUS And you will give me for them...how much gold?

ODYSSEUS No gold...but the drink of Dionysus.

SILENUS You say the nicest things: we're in desperate need.

ODYSSEUS Yes, and Maron, the son of a god, gave me the drink.

SILENUS Maron! (*telling another lie*) But I raised him in these arms of mine!..

ODYSSEUS (*sarcastically*) Oh yes? (*diplomatically*)...the son of Dionysus, as you clearly know better than I.

SILENUS Is the wine in your ship – or do you have it with you?

ODYSSEUS This wineskin, which you see, holds it, old man.

SILENUS That's not going to satisfy *my* thirst!

ODYSSEUS That's all I have with me.

SILENUS But do you have more on your ship?

ODYSSEUS Yes, twice as much as flows from this wineskin.

SILENUS A veritable fountain, which would be most welcome.

ODYSSEUS Would you like me, first of all, to give you a taste of this wine, unmixed?

SILENUS That's fair; and a taste encourages the purchase.

ODYSSEUS And I carry a cup along with this wineskin.

SILENUS Come; let it gurgle in, to remind me what drinking was like.

ODYSSEUS There you are.

SILENUS Mmmm! What a beautiful bouquet it has!

59

ODYSSEUS So you see how good it is!

SILENUS No, by Zeus, I can *smell* how good it is!

ODYSSEUS Taste it then; let your praise not be based on mere assumption.

SILENUS (*tastes the wine*) Oh yes indeed! Dionysus would have me dance! Mmmm!

ODYSSEUS It gurgles beautifully down your throat, does it not..?

SILENUS …to the tips of my fingers and toes!

ODYSSEUS I can pay you some gold as well.

SILENUS Just undo the wineskin. Forget the gold.

ODYSSEUS So then, bring out some cheese or a lamb.

SILENUS I will. Who cares about my master?! One cup, and I can feel a drunken frenzy coming on! For this wine, you can have all the flocks of every Cyclops! And I'll drive any left off the rocks into the sea! Just as soon as I've had a drink and relaxed my brow! Anyone who can drink and not be happy is mad! Drinking is a time for love's arousal – and breasts – and stroking beautiful hair – and dancing – and forgetting everything! So why should I not kiss this cup and let the stupid Cyclops and that eye in the middle of his head go hang?!

(*Exit* Silenus *into the cave*)

CHORUS Listen, Odysseus; we'd like to talk to you…

ODYSSEUS …as friend to friend.

CHORUS Did you take Troy – and that awful woman Helen?

ODYSSEUS Well, we sacked the city of King Priam.

CHORUS When you got hold of that woman, did you not all lie with her in turn, especially since she liked many husbands, the traitoress, who was struck with admiration at the sight of bright-coloured baggy eastern breeches on a man's legs and a golden band adorning his neck, and so left poor Menelaüs? The whole female sex should never have come into existence – except when they're in *our* company, of course!

(*Enter* Silenus *from the cave, bringing food*)

SILENUS   Look, King Odysseus; here is some shepherds' food for you: some lamb and plenty of cheese. Come, take them and leave the cave as quickly as you can – after giving me a cup of Dionysus' grape!
CHORUS   (*looking out of the cave*) Oh no! The Cyclops is coming!
What shall we do?!
ODYSSEUS   Where can we hide, old man?
SILENUS   Behind this rock. He won't see us there.
ODYSSEUS   A dangerous suggestion: we'll be in his nets.
SILENUS   It's not dangerous: there are plenty of escape routes through the rocks.
ODYSSEUS   No, no! Great Troy would groan if we were to run from a single man, when I have often stood behind my shield against countless Trojans! No! If we must die, let us die nobly – or live – but let us keep our reputation intact.

(*Enter* Cyclops. *On seeing him,* Silenus, Odysseus *and* Crew *hide behind the rock indicated by Silenus*)

[203]
CYCLOPS   Bring a light here! Hold it up!
(*A member of the Chorus brings and holds up a torch or lantern*)
What's all this frivolity, this Bacchic revelry?!

We'll have no Dionysus here, no bronze cymbals or noisy drums!

How are my lambs? Are they feeding with their mothers? And are the cheeses pressed in their wicker baskets?

Well, what have you to say for yourselves?

(*The Chorus remain silent, staring apparently unconcerned at the ground*)

One of you will soon be feeling the weight of my club! Look up, not down!

(*The Chorus all adopt various postures as they stare upwards*)

CHORUS See; we have raised our heads to Zeus himself. I myself am looking at the stars and Orion.

CYCLOPS Is my dinner ready?

CHORUS It is. You just need to have your appetite ready.

CYCLOPS And are the bowls full of milk?

CHORUS Yes, you can drink a whole jarful if you wish.

CYCLOPS Is it sheep's or cows' milk or a mixture?

CHORUS Whichever you want – just don't swallow me.

CYCLOPS I'll not do that – if I had you in my stomach, you'd stamp about and kill me with your posturing!

Hold on! Who's that I see by the sheep pens? Do we have pirates or thieves on our land? Anyway, I can see my sheep bound up with twisted saplings, and weapons hidden amongst the cheeses...

(*Silenus groans and appears, holding his head, apparently in pain*)

...and an old man's bald head battered and bruised.

SILENUS (*emerges from his hiding place*) Oh! My head feels like it's on fire! I've been beaten.

CYCLOPS By whom? Who's punched you on the head?

SILENUS (*pointing to Odysseus and Crew*) They have, Cyclops, because I wouldn't let them steal what was yours!

62

CYCLOPS Don't they know that I am a god descended from gods?

SILENUS I told them that! But they carried on stealing your property and eating your cheese, even though I wouldn't allow it, and carrying off your sheep! They said they would truss you up and put a collar on you, like a dog, with a three cubit leash; then they were going to gouge out your eyeball, and flay the skin off your back with a whip; then they were going to tie you to the benches of their ship when they set sail and sell you to someone to break rocks or to work at a mill!

CYCLOPS Is that so?! Perhaps you'd like to go now and sharpen the cleavers and knives and make a big fire from the woodpile? When I've slaughtered them, they'll soon be filling my belly, when I serve them as a hot meal straight from the charcoal, nicely boiled and tenderized in the cauldron! I'd like a change from my mountain-food: I'm tired of dining on lions and deer. It's time I had some human meat!

SILENUS Yes, something different from your usual fare would be more tasty, master. And we've had no strangers newly-arrived at our cave for a while.

ODYSSEUS Cyclops, listen in turn to us strangers. We are in need of food and we came from our ship to your caves to trade. This man sold us mutton in exchange for a cupful of wine, and he gave it to us as he took the drink – a willing seller and willing buyers. There was no question of force. This man has told you a pack of lies, and has been caught red-handed secretly selling your property.

SILENUS I?! May I die an evil death...

ODYSSEUS ...if I am lying?

SILENUS By Poseidon, your father, Cyclops! By the great Triton and Nereus! By Calypso and the daughters of

Nereus! By the sacred waves and every species of fish, I swear, o most excellent Cyclops, o master, that I did not sell your property to these strangers. May these poor children, whom I love above all else, die an evil death...

CHORUS Hang on! Speak for yourself! I saw you selling those things to the strangers! And if I'm not telling the truth, let my father die! You shouldn't be unfair to strangers.

CYCLOPS (*to Chorus*) You're lying. I trust him more than I would the Judge of the Dead, Radamanthus himself. He's an honest man.

But I have some questions.

Strangers, where have you sailed from? And where to? In what city were you raised?

ODYSSEUS I am from Ithaca. After sacking the city of Troy, we came to your land, Cyclops. We were driven here by stormy seas.

CYCLOPS So you're the ones who went to Troy, a neighbour of Scamander, to seek redress for the theft of that dreadful woman Helen?

ODYSSEUS We are; and we endured a terrible war.

CYCLOPS But it was a disgraceful expedition – to attack the land of Phrygia for the sake of one woman.

ODYSSEUS The gods instigated it: don't blame mortal men. But we pray of you, o noble son of the Sea God, and we speak freely:

Do not be so bold as to slaughter friends who come to your cave, or to put unholy meat to your lips.

We were the ones who established temples for your father to dwell in in the bays of Greek lands. The temples by the harbour of Cape Taenarum and in the hollows of lofty Malea remain inviolate. He has a safe home at the silver-bearing rock at Sunium, dedicated to Athene, and a refuge at Geraestus.

Further, it would have been a disgrace for us to give what belongs to Greece to the Phrygians. You are party to this, since you inhabit Greek land – here in the bays under the fiery rock of Etna.

Also, it is the custom of mortal men, even if you yourself see no reason for it, to welcome suppliants wrecked at sea, to afford them hospitality and to give them clothes, not to skewer them with ox-roasting spits and fill your mouth and belly with their fat thighs. And the land of King Priam has made a widow of Greece, drinking of the many war-ravaged corpses of the slaughtered, and rendered many wives husbandless, and old women and white-haired fathers childless. But if you eat up those who remain, and enjoy so cruel a feast, what hope for anyone is there?

Believe me, Cyclops; give up your gluttony. Let piety replace impiety. Remember: foul gain is so often answered with punishment.

SILENUS I'd like to give you some advice, Cyclops. When you eat him, don't leave anything. If you eat his tongue, you'll never be at a loss for words!

CYCLOPS Wealth, little man, is the god of the wise. All the rest is talk and elegant phrases. I care nothing for the temples by the sea in which my father dwells. Why do you boast of them? I do not shudder at Zeus' thunderbolts, stranger, nor do I know that Zeus is a greater god than I. I care nothing for the future. And listen to why I don't care. When from on high Zeus pours down his storms, in this cave I have dry covers; and when I have feasted on roasted calf or some other wild beast, and am lying back moistening my stomach drinking jugfuls of milk, I can easily rival Zeus' thunder with a blast from under my robe! And when the North wind blows snow from Thrace, I wrap my body in the skins of wild animals and light a fire, and so, snow is of no concern to me. The earth, of necessity, whether it wishes to or not, brings forth pasture to fatten my flocks, which I sacrifice to no-one except myself, and to no god except the greatest – this stomach of mine! To eat and drink thus from day to day and to suffer no hardship oneself – that is the god, the Zeus, of wise men! And those who introduce customs, prettifying men's lives, can go hang!

And so, I shall not cease from caring well for my soul – by eating you! Yes, you will accept that much hospitality, so that I meet your standards, by means of a fire and this my family's cauldron which will provide a shelter for your boiling, neatly-diced flesh. So, come further in, so that we can stand at the altar of the god of my home and you can entertain me sumptuously.

(*Exeunt* Cyclops, Silenus *and* Crew *into the cave*)

ODYSSEUS Ah! I have escaped the hardships of Troy and of the sea, but now I am held in the home of an unholy man who has a crude and inhospitable heart. O Pallas Athene, lady goddess daughter of Zeus, now, if ever, come to my aid! I am in the deepest danger, facing labours greater than those of Troy. And you, who live amongst the shining stars, Zeus, god of hospitality, look on us! And if you fail to see, you will be named differently – Zeus, god of nothing!

(*Exit* Odysseus *into the cave*)

SECOND CHORAL SONG

[356]
CHORUS   *[strophe]*
    O Cyclops open wide your lips
    and gaping gullet vast!
    Well-boiled and roasted, from the coals,
    are limbs of strangers, finely cooked
    in thick-fleeced goatskins fresh,
    for you to nibble and bite.
                    [mesode]
    But please, give none to me.
    This cargo is for you alone!
    Let pass such food as that;
    Let pass the Cyclops' offerings burnt
    on Etna's altars. Dine alone,
    delighting in the feast
    of strangers' meat.
                    [antistrophe]
    How merciless to sacrifice
    such suppliants at you hearth:
    to eat them, boiled, with loathsome teeth
    to chop them up and greedily
    them swallow, hot,
    as meat straight from the pot.

SECOND EPISODE

(Time: late the following morning)

(Enter Odysseus *from the cave, closing the cave door behind him)*

[375]
ODYSSEUS O Zeus, what am I to say? I have seen awful things inside the caves, unbelievable things, things one hears about but does not expect to see.
CHORUS What is it, Odysseus? Surely that unholy Cyclops has not eaten your dear friends for his dinner?
ODYSSEUS He picked out two of them, the ones with the most fat on them, prodding them with his fingers.
CHORUS Poor man, how could you all suffer so much?
ODYSSEUS When we came into the cave, the first thing he did was to light a fire, throwing broad tree-trunks of lofty oaks onto his hearth: their weight would be about three wagon loads. Then he placed a bronze cauldron on the fire. After that, he laid out his bed of loose pine fronds by the blazing fire. Having milked his cows, he filled a bowl with milk, pouring in about ten pitchers-ful. At its side, he placed an ivy-wood cup, – its breadth was about three cubits and its depth four – together with spits made of thorn, their points hardened in the fire and sharpened with a pruning-knife, and a bowl, forged on Etna, to catch the blood shed by his axes. When that god-hated sub-human butcher had made all ready, he grasped two of my comrades and killed them; then, with precise aim, he threw one of them into the hollow of the bronze cauldron and, seizing the other by the heel, struck him against a sharp pointed rock and smashed out his

68

brains. He cut off his flesh, slicing it violently with his knife, and roasted it on the fire, and then threw the limbs into the cauldron. Yet I had the presence of mind, though wiping a tear from my eye, to approach the Cyclops, – to serve him a drink. The others lay cowering, like birds, deep in the rocks, their skin drained of blood. And when he had had his fill of my comrades, he turned onto his back blowing air out through his mouth. Now, a brilliant idea had struck me. I filled a cup with Maron's wine and offered it to him, saying "Cyclops, son of the Sea God, take a look at this, a divine drink from the vines of Greece, the choice of Dionysus". And he, already sated with his disgusting meal, downed a long draught and was clearly impressed. Raising his hand, he said: "Dearest of strangers, to give me this beautiful drink to finish off a beautiful meal". When I saw that he had enjoyed it, I gave him another cupful, knowing that the wine could be his downfall and that he would soon pay the penalty. And so he did. He took to singing, and I poured him cup after cup to warm his belly – with drink. His tuneless singing mingled with the weeping of my shipmates: the whole cave echoed with the sound.

I left in silence. But I am willing to save myself and you, if you want me to. So tell me: do you want, or do you not, to flee this solitary man, and to live again in the halls of Dionysus with the Naiad nymphs? Your father inside supports my intentions, but he is weak and enjoys his drink: his mind is fuddled and his lips stick to the cup as if by glue. But you are young. Save yourselves as I do. Recover your old friend Dionysus. Be no servant of the Cyclops.

CHORUS Dearest friend, if only I could see the day when we escape from that godless Cyclops!

ODYSSEUS Listen then to my plan for revenge on this vile wild beast and for your escape from slavery.

CHORUS Tell me. For, the sound of no lyre anywhere in Phrygia could be sweeter than that of hearing of the Cyclops' death.

ODYSSEUS He'd like to go revelling with his Cyclops brothers now that he's had a taste of Dionysian wine.

CHORUS I see. So, you intend to wait by some desolate spot in the woods and take him and kill him or throw him down the rocks.

ODYSSEUS Nothing like that. My plan is more cunning.

CHORUS What is it then. We've often heard how clever you are.

ODYSSEUS Firstly, I'll keep him away from the revels by telling him he should not give such drink to other Cyclopes and that he should enjoy such of life's pleasures alone; but then, when he falls asleep, overcome by the wine... There is an olive branch in the cave which I can sharpen with my sword and put into the fire; when I see it's hardened, I'll lift it up, and I'll force it, still red-hot into the middle of the Cyclops' eye, which the fire will melt. And, just as a shipwright turns his drill using two straps, so will I twist and turn that fire-brand in the Cyclops' burning eye and destroy the eyeball.

CHORUS Yes, yes! I love your plan!

ODYSSEUS And then I'll get you, my comrades and the old man into the hull of my black ship and we'll set sail with double banks of oars.

CHORUS Is there any way that I could hold the torch that blinds his eye? It would be a kind of offering to our god.

ODYSSEUS In fact, I'll need you to. It's a big torch – not
    easily wielded.
CHORUS Even if it weighed a hundred wagon loads, I could
    still lift it, – if it meant that the eye of the Cyclops were
    to burn like a wasps' nest in a slow fire and the
    Cyclops were about to meet the end he deserves.
ODYSSEUS Be quiet now. You know the plan. When I tell
    you, follow my instructions. I have left my friends
    inside, but I shall not save only myself.

[Recitative with musical accompaniment]

[483]
CHORUS
    Who the first, the front line holding,
    ready to grasp the torch's handle,
    lift it up into the eye, yes,
    shining eye of Cyclops burning?
    Hush now, hush now! Mad with drinking,
    sings he such a din so graceless,
    out of tune, with such uncouthness,
    laid out in his cave, his shelter.
    Come now, let us teach him revels
    teach th' uneducated revels:
    he will soon be blind and eyeless!
                                    [strophe A]

    Blest is he who honours Bacchus,
    drinks at springs of wine belovèd,
    gives devotion to the revels,
    arm around a friend so carefree,
    on his bed a girlfriend lying,
    blonde luxurious hair anointed.
    Listen now! The Cyclops calls out:

71

CYCLOPS [1]
"Who will open me the door now?"

(*A member of the Chorus opens the cave door. Enter*
Cyclops, *drunk and holding a large wine cup, and* Silenus
*with the wineskin over his shoulder and carrying a wine-
bowl and a further cup*)

CYCLOPS   [*strophe B*]
    Ha ha ha ha! Full of wine, I
    shall enjoy the cheer of feasting,
    though my stomach's fit to bursting
    full to the deck its cargo carries.
    Cheerfully my load me beckons
    take my place at springtime revels,
    meeting Cyclopean brothers.
    Come you, bring my jar inside now.

CHORUS   [*strophe C*]
    Eyesight perfect now avails him;
    leaves he home, so fine appearing.
    Is there someone here to help us?
    Yes, an all-consuming fire-brand
    blazes for him. No nymph's wedding
    ever witnessed brighter torches,
    nor so many-coloured garland
    as will burst about his head.

(*Silenus sits down and places the wine-bowl and wineskin on
the ground close to himself*)

---

[1] The text gives the whole of strophe A to the Chorus.

ODYSSEUS Cyclops, listen! I am well acquainted with this
  wine of Dionysus which I have given you to drink.

CYCLOPS Who exactly is this Dionysus? Is it a god you
  speak of?

ODYSSEUS He's the greatest god to provide man with life's
  enjoyment.

CYCLOPS (*burping noisily*) Well, I certainly enjoy a good
  belch!

ODYSSEUS Yes, he's that kind of god; and he does no
  mortal man any harm.

CYCLOPS How can a god rejoice at having his home in a
  wineskin?

ODYSSEUS He's pleased to be wherever you put him.

CYCLOPS But should the gods keep their bodies inside
  wineskins?

ODYSSEUS Why not, so long as they provide you with
  pleasure? Or don't you like wineskins?

CYCLOPS I don't care for wineskins – but I do like the wine!

ODYSSEUS Stay here, and drink and be merry, Cyclops.

CYCLOPS But shouldn't I give some of this wine to my
  brothers?

ODYSSEUS If you're the only one to have any, you'll be
  held in higher regard.

CYCLOPS But it would be more generous to share it.

ODYSSEUS But drinking leads to arguments and fights.

CYCLOPS But I'm drinking now and no-one's laying a
  finger on me!

ODYSSEUS My dear Cyclops, it's always best to drink at
  home.

CYCLOPS But only a fool drinks and doesn't enjoy a bit of
  revelry!

ODYSSEUS But it's a wise man who drinks and stays at
  home.

CYCLOPS What shall we do, Silenus? Do you think I should
    stay here?
SILENUS I'd stay. Why do you need the others to share your
    drink?
ODYSSEUS And the ground here is lush and full of flowers.
SILENUS And it's lovely drinking in the warmth of the sun.
    Lie on the ground next to me.

(*As Cyclops sits and reclines, Silenus moves the wine bowl
within his own reach but behind Cyclops*)

CYCLOPS That's better. But why have you put the bowl
    behind me?
SILENUS I don't want anyone pinching it.
CYCLOPS You want to pinch it for yourself. Put it here in
    front of me! And you, stranger, tell me your name.

(*Silenus puts the wine bowl in front of Cyclops, but then moves
it to one side, within his own reach again*)

ODYSSEUS My name is Nobody. Are you going to help me
    now?
CYCLOPS Yes, I shall relieve you of the burden of your
    comrades – by dining on them!
SILENUS That's a fine example of hospitality, Cyclops.

(*Silenus turns his back on Cyclops as he drinks from the bowl*)

CYCLOPS You! You're secretly trying to drink my wine!
SILENUS No, no; it just kissed me for being handsome.
CYCLOPS You will regret it if you kiss the wine without it
    kissing you first!
SILENUS By Zeus, I wouldn't do that. It insists it's in love
    with my good looks.

74

CYCLOPS Pour some in here! And fill it up!

SILENUS But is it mixed properly? Let me check. (*takes a drink*)

CYCLOPS Hey you! Give me some!

SILENUS Not until I see you wearing garlands. I'll just have another sip (*takes another drink*).

CYCLOPS He's cheating!

SILENUS No I'm not. By Zeus, this wine is good! Now wipe your mouth before taking a drink.

CYCLOPS (*wipes his mouth*) There! My mouth and beard are quite clean now.

SILENUS Rest on your arm and have a drink as you see me have a drink (*drinks*) and as you don't see me (*drinks again as Cyclops adjusts his position*)

CYCLOPS Hey! What are you doing?

SILENUS I'm just draining this cup. (*drinks again, emptying his cup*)

CYCLOPS (*seizes the wineskin and gives it to Odysseus*) Stranger, take this. You can be my wine-bearer.

ODYSSEUS This wine and I are well acquainted.

CYCLOPS Pour me some.

ODYSSEUS Don't worry. No need to make a song and dance.

CYCLOPS Difficult not to when I'm drinking this stuff!

ODYSSEUS There; drink it; and don't leave a drop! When the cup's empty, you should be finished as well!

CYCLOPS This wine must have good timing, then!

ODYSSEUS And if you have a good drink with a good dinner, moistening your sated belly, it will send you to sleep; but if you leave any, Dionysus will leave you withered and parched!

CYCLOPS (*drinks deeply*) A narrow escape then! This is unbeatable stuff. The heavens seem to be mingled with the earth and I can see the throne of Zeus and the whole

75

holy array of the gods! I will not kiss them even though the Three Graces are tempting me! But enough of this! (*puts his arm around Silenus*) I have my Ganymede here who is more beautiful than the Graces. Who needs the female sex?!

SILENUS Am I then Ganymede, the son of Zeus, Cyclops?

CYCLOPS By Zeus, you certainly are, whom I have seized from Laomedon, your father!

SILENUS I'm done for, children! I think this is going to be unpleasant!

CYCLOPS Do you belittle your lover whilst enjoying his wine?

SILENUS I think this wine is going to have some nasty after-effects!

(*Exeunt* Cyclops *and* Silenus *into the cave.*)

ODYSSEUS Come now, noble children of Dionysus! The man is inside. He'll fall asleep but will soon be vomiting back his food. The fire-brand is inside the sheep pens and is smoking nicely. All that remains is to burn his eye out. Now is the time for each of you to show himself a man!

CHORUS Our courage is of rock or adamant! Go inside before our father suffers something terrible. Everything is ready for you.

ODYSSEUS Hephaestus, lord of Etna, let the eye of your evil neighbour burn brightly, and let us all then be done with it! And you, o Sleep, child of dark Night, fall unyielding on this god-hated beast, and do not allow Odysseus or his crew, after the glorious wars of Troy, to be destroyed by a man who cares nothing for either gods or mortals. Or else we must think that Chance rules the gods and that the gods are inferior to Chance.

76

(*Exit* Odysseus *into the cave*)

[Recitative with musical accompaniment]

[608]
CHORUS
> A pincer grip will seize the neck
> of him who dines on strangers' flesh,
> and soon by fire, his eyeball's light
> will quickly die.
> For, ready is the burning torch.
> A blazing branch of olive tree,
> lies hidden in the ashes hot.
> Let Maron's wine its part play well,
> the eye be lost, the drinking rued.
> And may I see my longed-for god,
> my Dionysus ivy-clad,
> and leave this barren Cyclops' land!
> Can this success be really mine?!

(*Enter* Odysseus *from the cave*)

[624]
ODYSSEUS (*speaking to the animals in the cave*) Quiet now,
> by the gods! You animals, keep calm: and keep your
> jaws together! I dare scarcely breathe, nor blink, nor
> clear my throat, in case I rouse that evil thing before
> the struggle of the Cyclops' eye be over.
CHORUS We're holding our breath.
ODYSSEUS Come along now! It's time to take hold of the
> torch in your hands: it's red-hot.

77

CHORUS   Tell us who should be first to take hold of the burning stake and burn out the Cyclops' eye: we're all in this together!

CHORUS (A)   (*moving away from the cave entrance and beckoning Chorus (B) forward*) We're rather too far from the door to reach his eye with the stake.

CHORUS (B)   (*all limping*) We each hurt our foot recently.

CHORUS (A)   (*all also limping*) We have the same problem; we sprained our ankles as we were standing here.

ODYSSEUS   You sprained your ankles as you were standing there?

CHORUS (A)   (*all limping and also rubbing their eyes*) And also we've got some dust in our eyes – or ash.

ODYSSEUS   You useless lot, you're no help at all!

CHORUS   Because I fear for my backbone and do not wish to have my teeth knocked out, am I therefore useless? However, I know an excellent magic spell used by Orpheus which will make the stake of its own accord approach his head and light a fire in that single eye of this son of the Earth.

ODYSSEUS   I began to understand your characters some time ago. Now I know for sure. I'll have to use my friends inside. Anyway, if your arms lack strength, at least you can cheer us on. Your encouragement will strengthen our resolve.

CHORUS   We're happy to cheer you on: and to have someone else fight our battles for us. So far as encouragement goes: "Blindness to the Cyclops!"

(*Exit* Odysseus *into the cave, leaving the door open*)

CONCLUSION

[Chant]

[656]
CHORUS
    Come on now – Noblemen;
    Burn his eye – eye of the –
    beast who feasts – strangers eats.
    Blind him oh! – Burn him oh!
    Shepherd of – Mount Etna!
    Twist the stake! – Careful be –
    lest in pain – dangerous he!

[663]
CYCLOPS (*from within the cave*) Ah!! My eye is burnt!!
CHORUS That's our victory song! Sing it again, Cyclops!
CYCLOPS Ah! Made a fool of and ruined! But even so, you can't escape through solid rock and you'll soon be laughing on the other side of your faces! You're nothing! I'm in the entrance of my cave and my hands will stop you!

(*Enter* Cyclops, *his eye burnt out, staggering in the entrance of the cave, flailing with his arms as if to stop anyone leaving.*)

CHORUS What are you shouting about, Cyclops?
CYCLOPS I'm done for.
CHORUS You certainly look to be in a mess.
CYCLOPS And in a sorry state also.
CHORUS Did you get drunk and fall into the fire?
CYCLOPS Nobody has destroyed me!
CHORUS Then no-one has done you harm.
CYCLOPS Nobody has blinded my eye!

79

CHORUS Then you are not blind.
CYCLOPS You shouldn't be so blind!
CHORUS How could nobody make you blind?
CYCLOPS Don't try to be clever! Where is Nobody?
CHORUS Nowhere, Cyclops.
CYCLOPS The stranger, I mean; that foul man who deluged me with drink!
CHORUS And Drink is a dangerous opponent and difficult to wrestle.
CYCLOPS By the gods, tell me – is he in the cave or has he got out?!
CHORUS They're being quiet and standing close to the rock.
CYCLOPS On which side?
CHORUS On your right.
CYCLOPS Where?
CHORUS Nearer the rock. Do you have them?
CYCLOPS (*bangs his head on the side of the cave*) Worse and worse! Now I've cracked my head open!

(*Cyclops has staggered forward, away from the cave entrance;*
Enter Odysseus *and* Crew *from the cave, making their escape.*)

CHORUS And now they *have* escaped!
CYCLOPS Where, where? Did you say over here?
CHORUS No, over there.
CYCLOPS Where?
CHORUS Keep going – on your left.
CYCLOPS Mockery! Disaster, and you mock me!
CHORUS They're not there now! And *he* is standing in front of you!
CYCLOPS You utterly evil man, where are you?!

80

ODYSSEUS I'm far enough away from you to keep my body safe – the body, that is, of Odysseus!

CYCLOPS What's that? Have you changed your name?

ODYSSEUS It's the name my father gave me. And you will continue to suffer for your unholy feast. It would have been a fine thing for me to sack Troy yet not avenge my comrades' deaths!

CYCLOPS Ah! The ancient prophesy is fulfilled! It said that I would be blinded by you on setting sail from Troy. But it also said that you would pay the penalty for this by being made to spend many a year wandering the seas.

ODYSSEUS Who cares about you and your prophecies?! I shall soon be at the headland and setting sail across the Sicilian Sea to my homeland.

CYCLOPS No, you don't! (*staggers about hopelessly*) Because I'll break off some rock and smash you and your shipmates with it! I might be blind, but I'll be up that hill to get a shot at you!

CHORUS We're shipmates of Odysseus now, and we'll be enslaved to Dionysus for the rest of time!

(*Exeunt* Odysseus, Crew, Silenus *and* Chorus *on their way to the ship.* Cyclops *collapses.*)